s

Proverbs 2:6, KJV

For the LORD gives wisdom; from his mouth come knowledge and understanding.

Proverbs 4:5 and 7, KJV

Get wisdom, get understanding: forget it not .... Wisdom is the principle thing; therefore get wisdom: and with all thy getting get understanding.

Printed in the United States of America
Library of Congress Cataloging-in-Publication Data

ISBN 978-0-578-96756-1

Published by JNF Enterprises, LLC.

Special discounts are available on bulk quantity purchases by book clubs, associations, churches and special interest groups.

For details:
email: glowt@earthlink.net or jnfenterprisesllc@gmai
l.com

Printed in the United States of America at Gorham

Printing, Inc

Dedication

This book is dedicated to my Sisters and Brothers In-Christ.

For the Word of God hath said, **"My people are destroyed for lack of knowledge… (Hosea 4:6, KJV)"** so, we are instructed in the Word of God to **"Cry after knowledge and lift up our voice for understanding (Proverbs 1:5, KJV)."**

We are told **"If any needs wisdom to know what you should do, you should ask God, and he will give it [Wisdom] to you…. (James 1:5, GWT)."**

So, ask Child of God so you might receive wisdom, knowledge, and understanding.

TABLE OF CONTENTS

Page

TABLE OF CONTENTS (cont'd)

PART 3
GUIDELINE STEPS

Page

TABLE OF CONTENTS (cont'd)

MY STORY

In the year of 1978, I had experienced many personal problems that had been building up in my life for several years. Due to the strain of these problems, I had begun to lose a lot of weight unbeknown to me that many of my co-workers had complimented on. But, because I never had a need to watch my weight, I wondered why my co-workers had noticed my weight loss and why I had not, nor had I felt a loss of weight in my body at that time.

During the week before I was to leave for the National Youth Convention, I had begun to feel the effects of the weight loss upon my body, and I began to feel sick. So, I had decided that I would check with my Doctor after I returned from the Convention for fear that this was just another one of Satan's ways of attacking me as he had done in the past before leaving for the Convention. So, I decided that whatever the problem was, I would not let anything get in my way of receiving the blessing I felt Jesus had promised me at the Convention.

While at work, I began completing all the tasks that needed to get done before I left for the Convention, and at that moment, I noticed in the office mail a departmental newsletter that had come around for all employees to read. As I sat down to read the newsletter, I noticed one of the subjects was about "Stress on the Job," and just as I began to read this article, I felt the move of the Spirit of God come over me as he had done so many times before and, I knew that God wanted to talk with me. So, I began to talk to God in my spirit and, I told him that I felt he wanted to say something to me concerning the newsletter I was reading. But, because I had so many things on my mind that I needed to

MY STORY (cont'd)

do before I left for the Convention, I felt that whatever God wanted to tell me, I could not receive it at that time. I asked God if he would wait until I got back from the Convention to talk to me. I did not realize at that time that God wanted to impart to me some knowledge about the "Stress" that was fighting against my body.

I said to God in my spirit that he had moved on me in this manner many times before and, each time, I felt he wanted to talk with me and impart something to me. So, if what I felt was really him moving on me, and I was not making a mistake in what I felt, I promised God that I would sit down and let him talk with me when I came back from the Convention. So, I sent the newsletter around for circulation to the other employees in the office to read, and I went to my Convention.

After I returned home from the convention, I went to the doctor and I talked with him about the problem of the weight loss and how I was feeling sick and, from the diagnosis of my Doctor's checkup, he stated that, he could not find the cause of my weight loss but, due to the things I explained to him that I was experiencing in my body, he stated that I was experiencing **"Stress."**

So, my Doctor recommended to me some "Stress Tablets" he felt would help me because the personal problems that I was having had started to seriously affect me, and all I wanted to do was to close my mind to the things that were troubling and worrying me. Later that day, after arriving back home, I took one of the "Stress Tablets" the Doctor recommended, and I went to bed just to close off my mind. The following morning when I woke up,

MY STORY (cont'd)

I opened my eyes, but I could barely see anything but a bright light that was shining in both of my eyes and, I did not understand what was happening to me. So, I left for work, and after arriving in my office, I sat down at my desk and suddenly began experiencing various emotional reactions within myself that felt very uncontrollable.

One of the feelings I felt was a sudden urge to scream and jump up from my seat. Not understanding what was wrong and, why I was experiencing these feelings, I decided I needed to leave work and go home for fear of what else would happen to me and what someone would think if they saw me reacting this way. So, I left work to go, and when I arrived home, I decided I needed to take one of the "Stress Tablets" that the Doctor had given to me because it relaxed my mind and helped me not to worry about my problems. So, I took one of the "Stress Tablets" and, I laid down and fell asleep. Later that evening, when I woke up, all the thoughts of my problems which were in my mind before I fell to sleep began to resurface and come back to my remembrance, and I could tell that the effects of the "Stress Tablet" was wearing off and, once again I thought to seek for relief by taking another "Stress Tablet" to calm my mind so I would not have to think about my problems.

When I realized that the "Stress Tablets" were actually calming my mind and causing me to forget about my problems, I realized that something had to be wrong if a pill could have that much effect to calm my mind from the troubling effects of my thoughts. So, I began to pray and talk with God about how I was feeling and, I told him I needed his help, I needed something to do,

MY STORY (cont'd)

something to occupy my mind so I would not think about my problems. As I prayed, I heard God say to me, "Go get a book and read it." I said, yes God that's right I'll get a book and read it, but I thought to myself, what book should I read? And, God said to me, "Get the encyclopedia." I said, alright God but, which one should I get? And God directed me to get the "Science Encyclopedia."

So, I got the Science Encyclopedia and, I turned to the index to determine what to read, and to my surprise, I found a topic entitled, "From Joy to Depression." This topic talked about the "Effects" of a specific "Stress Tablet" given to those who were experiencing Stress and how the tablet clears the mind of troubling thoughts. It told me why I could not remember my problems when I took the "Stress Tablets" and why I suddenly felt happy after taking the tablet because, the pills were so strong it actually erased from my mind the things I was worrying about.

After reading this topic, I realized what my problem was and the danger that my body was in and, I realized that what the Doctor had told me was true, that I was suffering from "Stress." So, I began to pray and ask God for his help because, as a child of God, I knew I was supposed to rely upon God and not a "Stress Tablet" for my help.

When I went back to work the next day, that same newsletter that I had circulated to the other employees in the office to read was sitting in the center of my desk. Suddenly, I remembered that earlier, when I saw this newsletter, I felt God wanted to talk with me to impart something to me. So, I began to pray within myself and, I told God that I remembered before I left to go to

MY STORY (cont'd)

the Convention, I felt that he had something he wanted to say to me and, I had promised him that I would let him talk to me when I returned from the Convention. Because I had felt this feeling many times before, I felt I needed to get a pencil and writing pad to write down what God had to say. As I sat down to read the article on "Stress on the Job," the spirit of God began to talk to me about the "Stress" that was fighting against my body and what I should do about it.

After I wrote down what God wanted to reveal to me about "Stress," I decided that I needed to write to my doctor and let him know what the "Stress Tablets" were doing to me. I told my doctor that I could no longer take the "Stress Tablets" that he had given to me because God had shown me what was wrong with me and, I realized I had to rely on God to help me deal with my problems as best I could. So, my doctor being a Jew, realized what I was saying to him, and he said to me, "I understand, Gloria, you do what you feel you need to do." So, after praying and asking God to help me with my "Stress problems," God spoke to my spirit and told me ***"Whenever I began to experience 'Stress' from the problems I was having, I was to 'get rid of it' and if I could not get rid of it, to give it to him and, he would move it for me."***

After God taught me through the writing he revealed to me about the **"Stress"** I was having the **"Stress"** simply vanished away and, God freed me from my **"Stress Situation"** and, I praise God for delivering me.

"When thou sad, seek ye my face, my heart said unto thee, thy face Lord will I seek."

(Psalm 27, verse 8)

MY TESTIMONY

I praise God for all the blessings he has bestowed upon me and for being so mindful of the things that go on in my life. For the Love of Jesus has so richly increased his blessings in my life, so much so, that he has been opening the doors to my prayers and giving to me those things that I have long been waiting for. Christ has broken my life many times and, in every break, I have learned more about my reasonable service as a child of God. And, in all of his breaking, he has given to me, through every test and trial, an inspirational writing which has carried me to higher heights and deeper depths of my faith in God. I am grateful to God for the trials that he has carried me through, which brought about this writing that he has allowed me to receive and, I would like to share that testimony with you in the hope that it will enrich and increase your faith, growth, and trust in God as it has mine.

At times I despaired of ever publishing this writing but, what kept me hoping was my desire to share with my Sisters and Brothers In-Christ this revelation knowledge that God shared with me about "Stress" so that the children of God will come to realize that, though we are the children of God, we are not immortal beings and, we must accept the reality that life does not eliminate us from going through the many "Stresses and Strains" of life.

MY TESTIMONY (cont'd)

This writing on "Stress" "What Stress is," "How it can be created and, "How it can affect us as Christians" is presented to God's people as a source of information to provide knowledge to help them understand the many things in life that can affect them.

In Hosea 4:6 (KJV), God tells us in his Word that, ***"My people are destroyed for lack of knowledge: because thou hast rejected knowledge...."*** And Proverbs 14:12, KJV says, ***"There is a way which seemeth right unto a man, but the end thereof are the ways of death."***

So as God's people, we need knowledge and understanding.

Ron Hembree, author of "Fruits of the Spirit," stated that, ***"Little things drive us to despair. Unresolved frustration so small...mounts until we are blinded to the path before us.... If we could learn the secret of instant access to God our endurance during "Stress" would be much greater"*** (Hembree, Ron, 1978, pp. 55 and 57).

So, I pray that, as you read this book on ***"Stress In the life of a Child of God,"*** that you will be blessed as you learn how to cope with or eliminate the ***"Stress"*** that you encounter in your life.

God Bless You.

PREFACE

The Word of God tells us in 1 John 1:8 says, "***If we say we have no sin we deceive ourselves and the truth is not in us (KJV).***" When we fail to admit to ourselves the truth about the ***"realities of life,"*** we lose the first opportunity to receive help with our problems. For instance, if a person is sick and they say they aren't sick or if an individual is dealing with an affliction in their body and deny that they have an affliction in their body, does that mean that the sickness or affliction does not exist? of course not and, so it is with the ***"Stresses and Strains of life."***

When an individual cannot admit to the ***"realities of life,"*** it does not negate the fact that the ***"realities of life"*** are real. But the individual in their refusal to admit to the ***"realities of life"*** can lose their first step in helping themselves deal with and resolve their life's problems."

PREFACE (cont'd)

2 Peter 1:2-3 (KJV) says, ***"According as his divine power hath given unto us all things that pertain unto life and godliness, through the knowledge of him that hath called us to glory and virtue…"***

MY TESTIMONY

Through my experiences while growing up in the church environment, I have witnessed Christians being taught that, because *"Death and life is in the power of the tongue"* (Prov. 18:21, KJV) Christians should be careful what they "say out of their mouth" because they were taught that, "they have whatever they say." Therefore, because of this teaching, when many believers are experiencing sickness or afflictions in their body, many would not admit that they were sick or that they had an affliction in their body, and because of this, they would reject the help of doctors and medication that could help them many times Christian would spiritualize these things away by saying that they were not sick, or the affliction does not exist and can't harm them in any way

PREFACE (cont'd)

MY TESTIMONY cont'd

because, for some Christians to admit to the "reality" of the sickness or affliction is like saying "they have no faith in God" and, this can be very despondent for some Christians. So, because many would refuse to admit to themselves that they were sick or that they had an affliction in their body, they would ignore the "reality" of the existence of these things in their body, and many of these individuals would not submit themselves to the help of doctors or medication.

Since Christians are not exempt from the ***"realities of life,"*** and life's ***"Stress Situations"*** we must realize that, as long as we live in a fallen world we will have to deal with the ***"realities of life"*** and life's ***"Stress Situations"*** but, we must look to God for his assistance in helping us deal with those realities.

PREFACE (cont'd)

Therefore, the **"Guideline"** in dealing with ***"Stress"*** provides the individual with steps to be performed that will help the individual discover a solution that will lead to solving, reducing, and coping with the ***"Stress Situation(s)"*** that may arise in their life.

A GUIDELINE FOR SOLVING AND COPING WITH STRESS SITUATIONS

INTRODUCTION

Mankind has in every span of life sought for a utopia world where they can live in a constant state of luxury, peace, and solitude of mind, free from the ***"Stresses and Strains"*** of life, and mankind has even gone to the far reaches of the world in search of this fulfillment. But, in all that mankind has done, they have found that

A GUIDELINE FOR SOLVING AND COPING WITH STRESS SITUATIONS

INTRODUCTION (cont'd)

wherever one goes, whatever one does, you can never escape from the **"Stressful Situations"** of life because one will either become irritated by people in one's world, aroused by one's own emotions from within or, bored by the non-activity of one's own life and no matter what one does, one will realize that there is always a state of unrest.

As people living in a technological age that is filled with many intricate and complex operations and workings of life, we tend to muddle through life frustrated, confused, and, perplexed looking for answers to our life problems.

There is a certain amount of ***"Stress"*** that comes into every individual's life that is necessary to keep an individual motivated and, the causes of that ***"Stress"*** can be pleasant or unpleasant and, *the effect that it has

A GUIDELINE FOR SOLVING AND COPING WITH STRESS SITUATIONS

INTRODUCTION (cont'd)

on the body will depend on how strong the ***"Effects of the Stress"*** is and the individual's ability to deal with it *****(Medical News Today article).***

MY TESTIMONY cont'd

During the tenure of my employment years, I worked for managers who had an excessive micro-management approach and attitude towards their employees, and I often suffered a lot of "Stress" in my employment." In one such position, I constantly dealt with a manager who had a micro-management approach and a dis-respectful way of talking to their employees. I was daily pressured and timed in completing my work assignments which created an excessive amount of "Stress" for me. One day while at work, I got up from my desk to go into the file room to xerox a document I was working on, and when I began to walk, my body began to retard itself. My brain was telling my body to move fast, but the message was not getting to my legs to move fast, and I could not move as

A GUIDELINE FOR SOLVING AND COPING WITH STRESS SITUATIONS

INTRODUCTION (cont'd)

MY TESTIMONY (cont'd)

quickly as I wanted to, and I was having pain on the right side of my body. At that moment, I realized that something was really wrong because I could not move as quickly as I wanted to. So, I informed my Manager that I did not feel well and needed to take leave. I called my sister and informed her what was wrong and asked her if she would come to pick me up and take me home because I feared falling down in the street because I could barely walk. That day, I made an appointment with my doctor for the following day.

After I went to the doctor he examined my reflexes and also sent me to take some X-rays of my body to find out what had happened to me. After my doctor examined me, he informed me that my reflexes were very slow and the X-rays showed that I had suffered a "muscular weakness or paresis" in my body, and he stated that I was suffering from an "Extreme 'Stress' disorder related to my work environment."

A GUIDELINE FOR SOLVING AND COPING WITH STRESS SITUATIONS

INTRODUCTION (cont'd)

The ***"*Effects* of *Stress"*** on the mind, the body and, the spirit of an individual can be very crucial if the individual allows the ***"Stress"*** to become so intense to the point that they are unable to function under its pressure because, some individuals will respond "physically" to ***"Stress"*** while others will respond "mentally and emotionally" to ***"Stress."***

"Stress" has become a universal concern of all of America and the number one health problem in life and the workforce. As children of God, sometimes we tend to respond to life in a cloudy, careless, and lackadaisical state of mind as though we are never affected by the things that go on in our world. Sometimes we ignore problems and situations that ***"Stress and Strain"*** us.

Sometimes we bottle-up our frustrations and disregard them as if it is taboo for the children of God to speak of

A GUIDELINE FOR SOLVING AND COPING WITH STRESS SITUATIONS

INTRODUCTION (cont'd)

such things or feel such effects. But, when the ***"Stresses and Strains"*** of life explode within us in the form of anger or frustration, and take a physical toll upon our lives, our mind and, our physical frame, then we see that the children of God are just as vulnerable to the ***"Stresses*** and ***Strains"*** of life that the people of the world are but, sadly as children of God we sometimes don't realize it until it results in our destruction and shame. As children of God when you find your life being affected by the ***"Stresses*** and ***Strains"*** of life, the Word of God tells us that we have an advocate who is Christ Jesus to whom you can go to and who will make intercession for us to help us with the resolution of our life's ***"Stresses*** and ***Strains."***

A GUIDELINE FOR SOLVING AND COPING WITH STRESS SITUATIONS

INTRODUCTION (cont'd)

MY TESTIMONY

In my young adult life, I dealt with a lot of frustration and heartache that I called "Stress" and, because of the heartache, the despondency, and the depressed feelings I felt so many times, I suffered with what" T. D. Jakes called "Silent Frustration." In his video entitled, "Overcoming Silent Frustration," he said:

> **"Buried beneath the smiles and professional demeanor of many people lurks an inner turmoil. It is a 'Silent Frustration. . . .' It comes in all colors, classes, and communities. It will attack even the very spiritual. When it is over frustration will turn to direction as God moves you systematically toward your destiny..., alleviate the stress and remove the pressure as you begin 'Overcoming Silent Frustration'."**

Because of the frustration and heartache, I held inside, I only felt secure enough to share it with my childhood girlfriend because, the heartache was so painful to me I did not want people to know the pain I was feeling or what I was *"Stressing"* over for fear of their judgment. So, I kept the frustration and the pain to myself, and I suffered *with "Silent Frustration."*

A GUIDELINE FOR SOLVING AND COPING WITH STRESS SITUATIONS

INTRODUCTION (cont'd)

Although there are many problems in life that the world, even the "Children of God" do not know how to solve or cope with, as I discuss the topic of ***"Stress," "What Stress Is," "How it can be created," "What it does," and "How it can affect one's life"*** we must realize that, the children of God have an advocate who is Christ Jesus to whom they can go to for the resolution of their life's **"Stresses and Strains,"** and he will make intercession for them and give them solutions to their problems. God will impart knowledge to the children of God and teach them how to understand and deal with their most intricate and complex workings of life to help them understand the things that pertain to their life and how to deal with them because nothing is too complex for God to impart to us, and nothing is above the power of God's ability to understand. This is why the Apostle Peter assures us in 2 Peter 1:3 (GNT) that

A GUIDELINE FOR SOLVING AND COPING WITH STRESS SITUATIONS

INTRODUCTION (cont'd)

"God has given us all things that pertain to life and godliness through the knowledge of him that hath called us to glory and virtue." Seeing that "we have all things that pertain to life and godliness," we ought to seek God for the wisdom and knowledge that he has that we lack in dealing with life's ***"Stresses and Strains."***

Then, whatever the child of God encounters in life, they will have every power, every ability, and every knowledge that is necessary to deal with life's **"Stresses and Strains"** because, it is God's 'Will' that his people be knowledgeable of the life he has given them so they might know and understand the life they are to live because God is knowledgeable in all things and, his knowledge is for the asking so, ask that you may receive.

So, as we discuss the topic of ***"Stress in the life of a Child of God,"*** we will compare it to the **"Stresses and**

A GUIDELINE FOR SOLVING AND COPING WITH STRESS SITUATIONS

INTRODUCTION (cont'd)

Strains" of life that many children of God and non-believers are faced with in their daily lives as they interact with the Church and the world.

The "Guideline for ***Solving and Coping with your Stress Situation(s)"*** is provided as a means of aiding you in becoming aware of some of the ***"Stressors"*** in your life that can lead to ***"Stress"*** and the ***"Effects"*** that ***"Stress"*** can have on one's life as well as, how to analyze whether or not they have ***"Stress"*** and, what they can do about it.

The total elimination of ***"Stress"*** is almost inevitable but, the cure for ***"Stress"*** is almost always successful. Using the ***"Guideline"*** can be helpful and, it is sure to be an excellent means of aiding one in solving and coping with their life ***"Stresses and Strains."***

A GUIDELINE FOR SOLVING AND COPING WITH STRESS SITUATIONS

INTRODUCTION (cont'd)

As you study the ***"Guideline for Solving and Coping with your Stress Situation(s)"*** and use it in correlation with the Word of God, I hope that you will learn how to apply the ***Guideline's instructions*** to the Word of God so you can find a **"Solution"** to help you change, eliminate or, reduce the ***"Stress"*** you are dealing with because many things in life can become ***Frustrating*** and ***Stressful*** to an individual's life but, God can teach and advise you through the instruction of God's Word what you, the Child of God, and non-believer can do about your ***"Stress"*** when it is created.

A GUIDELINE FOR SOLVING AND COPING WITH STRESS SITUATIONS

PART 1

WHAT IS STRESS?

WHAT DOES IT DO?

HOW DOES IT AFFECT YOU AND YOUR LIFE?

For the purpose of this book, I have determined ***"Stress"*** to be the ***"frustration of a given situation."*** Although ***"Stress"*** in and of itself is never something an individual would desire to experience but, like many things it can alert us to underlying problems. "Stress" can be an attention-getter, an activator and a motivator that can cause people to reassess their lives and situations and, it can be the 'stimulus'[1] that incites changes in one's life.

There is a certain amount of ***"Stress"*** that comes into every individual's life that is necessary to keep the individual motivated. The causes of that ***"Stress"*** can be pleasant or unpleasant and, the *"***Effect"*** that it has

A GUIDELINE FOR SOLVING AND COPING WITH STRESS SITUATIONS

PART 1 (cont'd)

on the body will depend on how strong the ***"Effect"*** of the ***"Stress"*** is and, the individual's ability to deal with it. The *** *"Effect"* of "Stress"** on the mind, the body and, the spirit of an individual can be very crucial if the individual allows the ***"Stress"*** to become so intense to the point that they are unable to function under its pressure because some individuals will respond "physically" to ***"Stress"*** while others will respond "mentally and emotionally" to ***"Stress."*** (*Felman, Adam. Stress: Why does it happen and how to manage it? *Medical News Today, 11/28/17*).

I believe there will always be a certain amount of ***"Stress"*** that God will allow to penetrate a Child of God's life to prompt the individual so they won't become sluggards in fulfilling God's Plan for their life; and to keep them motivated and inspired to perform his 'Will.'

A GUIDELINE FOR SOLVING AND COPING WITH STRESS SITUATIONS

PART 1 (cont'd)

There are many things in life such as Poverty,[2]

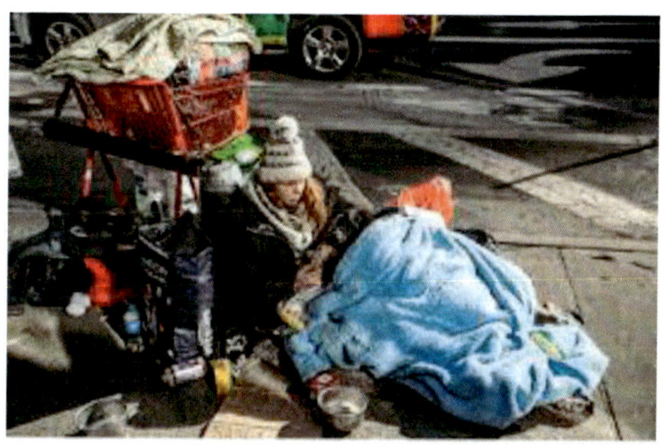

and depression, hunger, and distress, the need for love and friends, the lack of opportunities to help one succeed in life, the mismatch of one's abilities, the absence of the presence of God in one's life and, the lack of the fulfillment of

these things can bring about stressful situations that can frustrate one to no end and, make one's life difficult to cope with.

A GUIDELINE FOR SOLVING AND COPING WITH STRESS SITUATIONS

PART 1 (cont'd)

With that said let's go to the ***"Guideline for Solving and Coping with our Stress Situation(s)."***

In my discussion on the topic of ***"Stress,"*** I will use several hypothetical ***"Stress Situations"*** for ***"Shortcomings Within Oneself,"*** and ***"Mismatched Abilities"*** as they relate to the ***"lack of fulfillment"*** that the children of God, as well as the non-believer, can relate to. In these examples of ***"Shortcomings Within Oneself"*** and ***"Mismatched Abilities,"*** I will describe how ***"Stress"*** can be created in one's life through these examples and, I hope that you, the child of God, and non-believer will be able to relate to these hypothetical situations and apply the concept expressed in each example to your life's ***"Stress"*** problems to help you ***"Solve and Cope with your Stress Situation(s)."***

Also, we will look at what the ***"Guideline for Solving and Coping with Your Stress Situation(s)"*** suggest to help one

A GUIDELINE FOR SOLVING AND COPING WITH STRESS SITUATIONS

PART 1 (cont'd)

deal with their ***"Stress Situation(s)"*** because, when these ***"Stress Situation(s)"*** occur in one's life, many times the children of God tend to act as though they are immortal humans living in immortal bodies that are incapable of being affected by the destructive pressure and strain of ***"Stress."*** They tend to ignore their ***"Stress Situation(s)"*** as though it does not exist. Then, they try to spiritualize them away as if they have no effect or practical significance to their lives or could harm them in any way. Because, admitting to the reality of life's ***"Stress Situation(s)"*** for some individuals is very difficult. Therefore, when one does not admit to the realities of life, they lose the ***"First Step"*** to help solve their ***"Stress Situation(s)."***

This is why the ***"Guideline"*** provides ***Steps*** to be performed that will help the individual discover a ***"Solution"*** that will lead to solving, reducing and,

A GUIDELINE FOR SOLVING AND COPING WITH STRESS SITUATIONS

PART 1 (cont'd)

coping with their ***"Stress Situation(s)"*** that arise in their life. **When a person's values are much different than the value of the thing(s) they are a part of, there can be a feeling of ***"Stress,"*** and to be a part of something you don't want to be a part of or, if your ***"Ability"*** or ***"Abilities"*** is mismatched with the thing(s) you are doing, there can be a feeling of ***Stress"*** to do something you don't want to do but, to be a part of something you like to do can help an individual deal better with their ***"Stress.***

So, as we discuss ***"What Stress is," "What Stress does"*** and, ***"How Stress can affect you and your life."*** It is important to understand that ***"Stress"*** like many things can be a signal to "alert you. It can be an attention-getter, an activator and a motivator" that can cause people to reassess their lives and situations. It can also be the stimulus[3] that incites changes in one's life.

A GUIDELINE FOR SOLVING AND COPING WITH STRESS SITUATIONS

PART 1 (cont'd)

As I stated, ***"Stress"*** can be the ***"frustration"*** of doing something you don't want or like to do and, when you are "frustrated" by ***doing something that you don't want to do, that thing can create ***"Stress"*** in your life.

In an article published, April 2014 by author, Liz Makin, entitled, **"**How-Do-Your-Values-Impact -You-At-Work-Or- In-Your-Business"** it is stated that: "Where your values are aligned with your work or business you will find that they support and energise your work…." "It may be that some of your values are aligned, whereas others are not. If this is the case you will be happy with elements of your work but not others. The more you can align your values with your work or business the happier you will be in all areas of your life." "Where some or all of your values conflict with your work you are likely to feel very unsettled or stressed, e.g., …." "When you are feeling like this consider your values and look for ones that are currently conflicting with your work and then take action to change the situation."

http://makinithappen.co.uk/Articles/How-Do-Your-Values-Impact-You-At-Work-Or-In-Your-Business.html

A GUIDELINE FOR SOLVING AND COPING WITH STRESS SITUATIONS

PART 1 (cont'd)

MY TESTIMONY

After several years of working in a position that I loved and was a haven for me, due to the politics that was being played in this federal agency, my supervisor decided to resign his position, and this caused me to lose the position that I loved. So, I was reassigned to work in a different office and position. After several months of working in this new office and position, I was asked if I would accept a permanent position with this office but, because of the extreme "Stress" I suffered that took a devastating toll on my body while working in this office, I refused the offer, and I was once again transferred to another office and position. This time, I was transferred to another office and placed in an entry-level position that I had not been trained for, and I was downgraded because I was told I could not occupy that position at the grade level I was at because my grade was too high for that position. This presented a whole new ball of problems for me and, I was "Stressed" and angered because I had worked hard to get to the grade I was at and, I was greatly disappointed

A GUIDELINE FOR SOLVING AND COPING WITH STRESS SITUATIONS

PART 1 (cont'd)

MY TESTIMONY cont'd

that my Agency would place me in an entry-level position at my grade level.

After working in this new position, a year later, my new Manager resigned, and another Manager was hired in their place. Because I was a trainee in this new position, the second Manager realized I was not very skilled in my job even though the former Manager told her I was.

So, when the new Manager began to question me about my work, I informed her I was being trained in this position but, she felt I was lying about not knowing my job, and this created constant badgering and threats of demotion and, I became very angry and frustrated each day with my new Manager, and I began to experience an extreme amount of "Stress." So, I went to the Executive Director of the Agency and asked for a reassignment to a different position but, he would not grant it.

A GUIDELINE FOR SOLVING AND COPING WITH STRESS SITUATIONS

PART 1 (cont'd)

MY TESTIMONY (cont'd)

So, I prayed about the situation and, God moved in his own way. Instead of allowing me to be moved to a different position, God allowed a conflict to arise with my Manager and the Head of the Agency, and it also affected the position of the Executive Director. Eventually, they both resigned from their jobs, and God gave me a temporary relief from the "Stress" that my Manager was causing me.

As I stated in the previous article by author Liz Makin, **"Where some or all of your values conflict with your work you are likely to feel very unsettled or stressed...."** So, as I stated, ***"Stress"*** can be the ***"frustration"*** of doing something you don't want or like to do and, when you are ***"frustrated"*** by **<u>doing something that you don't want to do</u>, that thing can create ***"Stress"*** in your life.

A GUIDELINE FOR SOLVING AND COPING WITH STRESS SITUATIONS

PART 1 (cont'd)

As we discuss "What Stress is," "What it does," and "How it can affect your life," we will discuss a **"Hypothetical Situation"** dealing with **"Mismatched Abilities"** as it relates to the ***"lack of fulfillment"*** and how this ***"lack offulfillment"*** can create ***"Stress"*** in one's life.

In this **"Hypothetical Situation"** of **"Mismatched Abilities,"** I will refer to things that one is doing that are a ***"Mismatch"*** of one's ***"Ability(ies)."*** With that said, let's go to the ***"Guideline for Solving and Coping with Stress Situations"*** in reference to our **"first"** example of **"Mismatched Abilities."**

A GUIDELINE FOR SOLVING AND COPING WITH STRESS SITUATIONS

PART 2

- **<u>HYPOTHETICAL SITUATION NO. 1</u> – *<u>MISMATCHED ABILITIES</u>**

In this "Hypothetical Situation" of **"Mismatched Abilities"** let's say you are a ***"Child of God"*** in the church and, you have the ***"Ability"*** to play the piano, direct the choir and, compose songs but, you are not operating in these ***"Abilities"*** instead, you are just singing on the choir or, just idly sitting by and you are beginning to feel a ****"***lack of fulfillment."*** If you have the desire to function in your ***"Ability(ies)"*** and, you are not doing so, you can become ***'frustrated'*** and even depressed because, your ***"Ability(ies)"*** is being ***"Mismatched"*** with the thing(s) you are doing and, your desire to be fulfilled in your ***"Ability(ies)"*** is not being achieved resulting in your ***'lack of fulfillment'*** can create a feeling of ***"Stress"*** within you.

A GUIDELINE FOR SOLVING AND COPING WITH STRESS SITUATIONS

PART 2 (cont'd)

❑ HYPOTHETICAL SITUATION NO. 1 – MISMATCHED ABILITIES (cont'd)

Now if your need to be fulfilled in your ***"Ability(ies)"*** becomes so strong a desire and obsession within you that you become dissatisfied with the present state and condition of your life then, you can begin to conceive thoughts of yourself performing in your ***"Ability(ies)."*** These thoughts of your desire and personal need to be fulfilled in your ***"Ability(ies)"*** can become such a strong emotional desire within you that, you can become irrational in your thinking and actions. What I mean by that is, you can become unreasonable or insensitive in the things that you say or do because, your mind is constantly preoccupied with the thoughts of fulfilling your desire and working in your ***"Ability(ies)."***

A GUIDELINE FOR SOLVING AND COPING WITH STRESS SITUATIONS

PART 2 (cont'd)

- **HYPOTHETICAL SITUATION NO. 1 - MISMATCHED ABILITIES (cont'd)**

You might even reach the point where you are constantly living in a daydream or fantasizing state of mind.

Physically, you may still be hanging around the church or, you may decide to leave the scene altogether. So, you may ask yourself the question, "How can this happen to an individual?" It can happen when an individual's ***"Ability(ies)"*** is ***"Mismatched"*** with their present situation and when their desire is unfulfilled resulting in their need(s) not being met.

Researchers have discovered that, many times when an individual's ***"Ability(ies)"*** is ***"Mismatched"*** and they are **"unfulfilled"** ***"frustration"*** will set in and ***"Stress"*** will follow and the individual may cop-out mentally or,

A GUIDELINE FOR SOLVING AND COPING WITH STRESS SITUATIONS

PART 2 (cont'd)

❑ HYPOTHETICAL SITUATION NO. 1 - *MISMATCHED ABILITIES (cont'd)

physically drop-off the scene altogether. Remember, some people react to ***"Stress"*** physically and some people react to ***"Stress"*** mentally and emotionally.

As we look at this philosophical concept applied in the above Hypothetical Situation, we can see how there can be many individuals both in the

Church and in the world that have become discouraged, frustrated, and depressed with their life situation(s)

A GUIDELINE FOR SOLVING AND COPING WITH STRESS SITUATIONS

PART 2 (cont'd)

❑ **HYPOTHETICAL SITUATION NO. 1 – MISMATCHED ABILITIES (cont'd)**

because of their *"*lack of fulfillment* and *"Mismatch Abilities."* In the past, this is the reason why many **"*Institutions and Corporations"** developed all kinds of motivational and incentive programs for their employees to help them reach their employment goals and ambitions, and to give them an opportunity to be fulfilled in their careers and positions to help them become better productive employees and, it is also true with the "Child of God" in the Church. Churches have begun all types of programs to entertain the members of the church (the body of Christ) so they can feel fulfilled in their churches.

As children of God, the Word of God tells us in 1 Corinthian 12 verse 7 that, ***"the manifestation of the Spirit is given to every man to profit withal"*** [4] because it is also

A GUIDELINE FOR SOLVING AND COPING WITH STRESS SITUATIONS

PART 2 (cont'd)

- **<u>HYPOTHETICAL SITUATION NO. 2</u>** – **<u>SHORTCOMINGS</u>**

"God's Will" for his Children to prosper in their "gifts" and "Abilities" that he has given to them for the upbuilding and edification of the "Body of Christ" so they may profit in the use and operation of their gifts for their ***"fulfillment"*** in the Church. This is also why the Word of God says, ***"God has given unto us all things that pertain to life and Godliness.***[5] ***"***

So, as we look at this hypothetical situation and we consider the reason for God's intended purpose for his children, it is important that an individual's "gifts" and **"Ability(ies)"** be developed, fulfilled, and equally matched with their present involvement or situation(s) in life otherwise, as it has always been and will continue to be, people will go out in search for that place or thing

A GUIDELINE FOR SOLVING AND COPING WITH STRESS SITUATIONS

PART 2 (cont'd)

❑ HYPOTHETICAL SITUATION NO. 2 – SHORTCOMINGS

that will bring them the opportunity for their ***"fulfillment."***

Let's look now at another ***"Hypothetical Situation."*** This time we will deal with the subject of ***"Shortcomings Within Oneself."*** We will use the position of a church **"Worship and Praise Leader"** as it relates to the responsibilities of that position.

Now, this activity may be very ***"Stressful and frustrating"*** for some individuals and, you may ask yourself the question, ***"In what way can this be stressful and frustrating?"*** Hypothetically speaking, the ***"Stress"*** of this position can be created by several things, (1) Your lack of experience as a **"Worship and Praise Leader"** (2) Your inability to sing songs that can lead a

GUIDELINE FOR SOLVING AND COPING WITH STRESS SITUATIONS

PART 2 (cont'd)

- **HYPOTHETICAL SITUATION NO. 2 – SHORTCOMINGS (cont'd)**

congregation into a "worship and praise" state of mind and, (3) The inability to "motivate oneself" as a **"Worship and Praise Leader"** to perform in this function and, there could also be a number of other reasons that could keep an individual from performing effectively in this position as a **"Worship and Praise Leader."**

Now, as a **"Worship and Praise Leader"** if you the individual are unsuccessful in performing in this type of position to motivate and encourage the congregation to get involved in the **"Worship and Praise Service"** then, the function of this position can become ***"Stressful and Frustrating"*** to you. It can also cause you to develop a dislike for the position as a **"Worship and Praise Leader"** because of the ***"Stress and Frustration"***

A GUIDELINE FOR SOLVING AND COPING WITH STRESS SITUATIONS

PART 2 (cont'd)

❑ HYPOTHETICAL SITUATION NO. 2 – SHORTCOMINGS (cont'd)

of the position. You may also develop an unpleasant personality within yourself created by the ***"Stress"*** of the position, and when this begins to happen to you, you may begin to feel a ***"Mismatch of your Ability(ies)"*** and a ***"Shortcoming(s) Within Yourself."***

The outcome of the above ***"Hypothetical Situation"*** is to show how dealing with 'people' for some individuals can be more **"stressful"** than dealing with 'things' but, it can also show how dealing with 'things' for some individuals can be less **"stressful"** than dealing with 'people.'

So, let's look at what the **"Findings"** would be for this "***Hypothetical Situation No. 2***."

When we look at the findings of this ***"Hypothetical***

A GUIDELINE FOR SOLVING AND COPING WITH STRESS SITUATIONS

PART 2 (cont'd)

- ❑ **<u>FINDINGS FOR HYPOTHETICAL SITUATION NO. 2</u>**

Situation" dealing with ***"Stress,"*** one of the things we should learn from this example is, "to be aware of any and all existing problems or situations that can cause you ***"Stress"*** and, determine whether or not the problem(s) of the ***"Stress"*** is **"<u>internal</u>"** or **"<u>external</u>"** to yourself and, whether or not the problem(s) of the ***"Stress"*** is due to a ***"Shortcomings within Oneself"*** or a ***"Mismatch of one's Ability(ies)."*** To ignore the ***"Stress"*** in the situation you are dealing with, and any of the things that could be causing you ***"Stress"*** would be unwise because, when you the individual begins to experience ***"Stress"*** in any given situation and you ignore the ***"Stress"*** by refusing to believe and accept the reality that, a ***"Stress Situation"*** exists in your life, you can begin to function in a **"State of Denial"** which can

A GUIDELINE FOR SOLVING AND COPING WITH STRESS SITUATIONS

PART 2 (cont'd)

❑ FINDINGS FOR HYPOTHETICAL SITUATION NO. 2 (cont'd)

only cause the problem of your ***"Stress"*** to increase and, eventually the ***"Stress"*** can become very detrimental to the individual's spirit and affect the healthy personality and frame of mind of the individual and later cause an even greater problem.

This is why the ***"Guideline for Solving and Coping with Stress Situation(s)"*** advises one to ***"First"*** be willing to ***"Recognize the Problem and Acknowledge the Existence of the Stress Situation(s)"*** and, do not ignore the ***"reality"*** of the problem as if it does not exist because, this is ***"Step No. 1"*** in helping an individual learn how to deal and cope with their ***"Stress Situation(s)."***

A GUIDELINE FOR SOLVING AND COPING WITH STRESS SITUATIONS

PART 2 (cont'd)

- ### <u>FINDINGS FOR HYPOTHETICAL SITUATION NO. 2</u> (cont'd)

Now, let's substantiate the advice given in ***"Hypothetical Situation No. 2"*** as it relates to ***"Step No. 1, Recognize the Problem and Acknowledge its Existence."***

Then, we will compare the ***"Guideline for Solving and Coping with Stress Situations"*** with the **"Word of God"** using the biblical reference below.

When the Apostle Paul examined the ***"Stress Situation"*** that he was faced with in his life, he ***"Recognized and Acknowledged"*** that his ***"Stress Situation(s)"*** was caused by a ***"Shortcoming"*** and an ***"Inability Within him."***

The **"Guideline"** states in ***"Step No. 1,*** to ***"Recognize the Problem and Acknowledging the Existence of the Stress Situation(s)"*** in one's life. It does not matter whether it is a church situation or a personal life situation.

A GUIDELINE FOR SOLVING AND COPING WITH STRESS SITUATIONS

PART 2 (cont'd)

❑ **FINDINGS FOR HYPOTHETICAL SITUATION NO. 2 (cont'd)**

You may also have to ***"Acknowledge"*** that, there may be a ***"Shortcoming or Inability Within You"*** or a ***"Mismatch of Your Ability(ies)"*** that is causing a ***"Stress"*** in your life and, you may also have to recognize and acknowledge your need for God and, the problem(s) of your life without God.

❑ **BIBLICAL REFERENCE - ROMANS 7:14-21, THE STRUGGLES OF THE APOSTLE PAUL**

The Apostle Paul "Recognized the Problem and Acknowledged the Existence of a "Stress Situation(s)" existing in his life, and he gives us an excellent example of how he dealt with his "Stress Situation(s)." This example can help an individual to "Recognize the Problem and Acknowledge the Existence" of a "Stress Situation(s)" that exists in their life.

A GUIDELINE FOR SOLVING AND COPING WITH STRESS SITUATIONS

PART 2 (cont'd)

- **BIBLICAL REFERENCE - ROMANS 7:14-21**

Now, we realize that, in the Apostle Paul's day and time, that he did not refer to his life situation(s) as ***"Stress"*** instead, he called his situation(s) a **"Struggle"** within himself and a **"Warfare"** of his mind. Paul felt he was trapped in a situation(s) he did not have the ability to handle but, he did not ignore or deny the fact that he had a ***"Stress Situation(s)"*** existing in his life, and that it was causing him "Stress." Neither did Paul ignore or deny his ***"Shortcomings" or "Inability"*** to solve and deliver himself from his ***"Stress Situation(s)."***

Therefore, Paul accepted the reality of the ***"Stress Situation(s)"*** that existed in his life and, he asked himself the question, ***"Who can deliver me from the body of this death.[6]"***

Let's go now and study the **"Guideline's Steps."**

A GUIDELINE FOR SOLVING AND COPING WITH STRESS SITUATIONS

PART 3

"GUIDELINE STEPS"

❑ STEP NO. 1 - RECOGNIZE THE PROBLEM AND ACKNOWLEDGE ITS EXISTENCE

Now, the Apostle Paul in ***"Recognizing and Acknowledging the Stress Situation(s)"*** that existed in his life, also ***"Acknowledged"*** his ***"Inability(ies)"*** to deliver himself from the frustration and strain of his ***"Stress Situation(s)"*** so, he declared himself to be an "Old Wretched Man."

MY TESTIMONY

I have learned through many of my life experiences that, "Stress (frustration)" is not something that is easy to deal with. It can be created from things like, financial strain, people's negative criticism, negative attitudes, and negative reactions towards an individual that can bring on feelings of Stress, sadness, heartache, and depression. It can also cause an individual to

A GUIDELINE FOR SOLVING AND COPING WITH STRESS SITUATIONS

PART 3

"GUIDELINE STEPS"

- ❑ **STEP NO. 1 - <u>RECOGNIZE THE PROBLEM AND ACKNOWLEDGE ITS EXISTENCE</u> (cont'd)**

MY TESTIMONY (cont'd)

want to withdraw from dealing with people and life. There were times in my life where I just wanted to get away from people and family to stop the heartache they caused me because of their criticism and negative attitudes expressed towards me.

I even thought at times about moving away, and I even entertained the thought of joining a convent just to get away from it all. This is why through all of the "Stress Situations" I have dealt with in my life, God has instructed me to "Get Rid of It" or "Give It to Him and He would get rid of it for me."

A GUIDELINE FOR SOLVING AND COPING WITH STRESS SITUATIONS

PART 3

"GUIDELINE STEPS"

❑ STEP NO. 1 - RECOGNIZE THE PROBLEM AND ACKNOWLEDGE ITS EXISTENCE (cont'd)

MY TESTIMONY (cont'd)

So, in many of the "Stress Situations" I have experienced, I have done just that as often as I could, even when it meant separating myself from situations that were causing me "Stress" and from doing things with individuals who caused me "Stress."

Paul knew that he would not be able to deliver himself from his ***"Stress Situation"*** so he wanted to know ***"Who will deliver him?"*** He asked for help from someone who had no ***"Shortcomings or Inabilities"*** to help him and, that someone was Christ Jesus. Paul ***"Acknowledged"***

A GUIDELINE FOR SOLVING AND COPING WITH STRESS SITUATIONS

PART 3

"GUIDELINE STEPS"

❑ STEP NO. 1 - RECOGNIZE THE PROBLEM AND ACKNOWLEDGE ITS EXISTENCE (cont'd)

the reality of the ***"Stress Situation(s)"*** in his life and, he was able to accept and not ignore the things that were happening to him because, it was the Apostle Paul who said, ***"We are troubled on every side yet not distressed, we are perplexed, but not in despair, persecuted, but not forsaken, cast down, but not destroyed (2 Corinthian 4:8-9, KJV).***[7]***"*** The Apostle Paul took the ***"First Step"*** recommended by the **"Guideline"** to ***"Recognize the Problem and Acknowledge the Existence"*** of a ***"Stress Situation(s)"*** existing in his life and, you too must ***"Recognize the Problem and Acknowledged the Existence"*** of the ***"Stress Situation"*** in your life. Then, ***"Step No. 2"*** in the ***"Guideline"*** advises one to ***"Seek the***

A GUIDELINE FOR SOLVING AND COPING WITH STRESS SITUATIONS

PART 3

"GUIDELINE STEPS"

❑ STEP NO. 1 - RECOGNIZE THE PROBLEM AND ACKNOWLEDGE ITS EXISTENCE (cont'd)

Whereabouts of the Stress" and, ask yourself the question, ***"Where is this "Stress" coming from?"***

Paul recognized the frustration and strain of his ***"Stress situation(s)"*** and, he ***"Acknowledged"*** the problem of his ***"Shortcoming(s) and Inability"*** to help himself and, he admitted his need for help from God who had no shortcomings. Once you have performed ***"Step No. 1"*** to ***"Recognize the Problem and Acknowledge the Existence of a "Stress Situation"*** in your life then, ***"Step No. 2"*** of the ***"Guideline"*** advises you to ***"Seek the Whereabouts of the Stress"*** and ask yourself the question, ***"Where is this Stress coming from?"***

A GUIDELINE FOR SOLVIING AND COPING WITH STRESS SITUATIONS

PART 3

"GUIDELINE STEPS"

❑ **STEP NO. 1 - <u>RECOGNIZE THE PROBLEM AND ACKNOWLEDGE ITS EXISTENCE</u> (cont'd)**

So, let's look now at "***Step No. 2" "Seek the Whereabouts of the Problem"*** using the same Biblical Reference in Romans 7:14-21.

❑ **STEP NO. 2 - <u>SEEK THE WHEREABOUTS OF THE PROBLEM</u> (cont'd)**

When you seek the ***"Whereabouts" of your Stress Situation(s)"*** you should determine where your ***"Stress"*** is coming from. Is it ***"<u>internal</u>"*** or ***"<u>external</u>"*** to yourself? Or is it a ***"Mismatch of your Ability(ies)"*** in your present situation?

❑ **<u>BIBLICAL REFERENCE – ROMANS 7:14-21</u>**

In Romans 7:15-21 (GNT), the Apostle Paul stated,

A GUIDELINE FOR SOLVING AND COPING WITH STRESS SITUATIONS

PART 3
"GUIDELINE STEPS"

❑ **BIBLICAL REFERENCE – ROMANS 7:14-21**

"I do not understand what I do. For what I want to do I do not do, but what I hate I do.*[9]*" Paul found that he was struggling with a **"warfare"** that was going on within himself and, he was ***"frustrated"*** with doing something he did not want to do and, allowing himself to be brought into captivity to it. So, he **"warred"** against the law of his mind of how to free himself from the ***"Stress Situation(s)"*** existing in his life, and he found that, the ***"Whereabouts of the Stress Situation(s)"*** that caused him his ***"Stress"*** existed within him.

Paul said, ***"I am carnal, I am sold under sin . . . and within my members, I find another 'Law' (a rule of conduct) warring against the law of my mind.*[8]*"***

A GUIDELINE FOR SOLVING AND COPING WITH STRESS SITUATIONS

PART 3

"GUIDELINE STEPS"

- ❑ **STEP NO. 2 - SEEK THE WHEREABOUTS OF THE PROBLEM (cont'd)**

- ❑ **BIBLICAL REFERENCE – ROMANS 7:14-21**

So, because Paul could not free himself from the ***"frustration"*** and ***"Strain"*** of his ***"Stress Situation(s),"*** he experienced the "Stress" of being brought into captivity to things he did not want to do. The Apostle Paul was limited in many situations that he could not free himself from and he found himself bound by the limitations and restraints of his situation(s) and, these limitations and restraints caused him ***"Stress."***

So, in comparison to Paul's **"Warfare"** example, if you find you are being brought into captivity or subjection to something you don't want to do, it does not necessarily mean that you are held totally and helplessly bound against your 'Will' but, it can mean

A GUIDELINE FOR SOLVING AND COPING WITH STRESS SITUATIONS

PART 3
"GUIDELINE STEPS"

❑ STEP NO. 2 - SEEK THE WHEREABOUTS OF THE PROBLEM (cont'd)

that you are drawn in weakness to something or, you are restrained and limited in a situation that you are a part of that you cannot free yourself from that is causing you ***"Stress."*** Let's look now at the ***"Hypothetical Findings"*** for the ***"Step No. 2."***

❑ HYPOTHETICAL FINDINGS

When you look at the ***"Stress Situation(s)"*** existing in your life, and you have determined that you are doing things you really don't want to do, and are not doing the things that you want to do, and you hate the things you have to do, you may find like the Apostle Paul that, the ***"Whereabouts of your "Stress"*** is a **"Struggle"** that is going on within you or, with the things you are doing

A GUIDELINE FOR SOLVING AND COPING WITH STRESS SITUATIONS

PART 3

"GUIDELINE STEPS"

- **STEP NO. 2 - <u>SEEK THE WHEREABOUTS OF THE PROBLEM</u>**

- **<u>HYPOTHETICAL FINDINGS</u> (cont'd)**

and are limited in doing and, these things are causing you ***"Stress"*** and a **"warfare"** in your mind. When you are brought into captivity to do things that you don't want to do a **"Struggle"** in your mind caused by the ***"Stress Situation(s)"*** can create an enormous amount of ***"Stress"*** that can cause strong stressful effects within you, and you can become ***"frustrated"*** and dissatisfied with your present situation(s) because you are struggling with things you don't want to do. When these things begin to happen to you, the ***"Guideline"*** advises one to go to ***"Step No. 3"*** and look at the ***"Effect(s)*** the ***"Stress"*** is having on you.

A GUIDELINE FOR SOLVING AND COPING WITH STRESS SITUATIONS

PART 3
"GUIDELINE STEPS"

❑ STEP NO. 3 - EFFECTS OF THE STRESS

Although Paul in the seventh chapter of the book of Romans was speaking of the ***"Effects(s)"*** that sin can have on an individual to cause them to do what they don't want to do when they are brought into captivity to it that same analogy of **"Captivity"** can still be used in determining how the ***"Effect(s) of Stress"*** can work in an individual who is brought into ***"Captivity"*** to continually do things that one does not want to do, and when these things happen to you, you must look at the ***"Effect(s) of the "Stress"*** is having on you and what it's causing you to do. Is it causing you to become tangled up in a **"Warfare"** of your mind? When one becomes wretched one can react in a distasteful and dissatisfied manner, and you can easily become irritated or agitated and even hostile because you have become tangled up

A GUIDELINE FOR SOLVING AND COPING WITH STRESS SITUATIONS

"GUIDELINE STEPS"

❑ STEP NO. 3 - EFFECTS OF THE STRESS (cont'd)

in a **"Warfare"** of your mind, the **"Warfare"** of how to free yourself from your ***"Stress Situation(s)."*** Is it causing you to react in a distasteful manner? The Apostle Paul said it made him **"An Old Wretched Man."**

The ***"Effect(s) of the Stress"*** can cause you strong stressful effects in your body because the pressure of the

MY TESTIMONY

I have found in my dealing with the "Stress Situations" in my life that, if "Stress" is not dealt with it can cause you devastating feelings and emotions within yourself that you may not like. As I dealt with some of the criticism and negative attitudes directed toward me, I found that I developed hate in my heart towards those individuals and, because of this hate I began to feel miserable, and I did not want to have much to do with them.

A GUIDELINE FOR SOLVING AND COPING WITH STRESS SITUATIONS

"GUIDELINE STEPS"

❑ STEP NO. 3 - <u>EFFECTS OF THE STRESS</u> (cont'd)

In Paul's example, it is concluded that, when these things happen to you it is no more you reacting but, it is the ***"Effect(s)"*** of the ***"Stress"*** within you **'warring'** against the law of your mind and creating in you an irritation of your spirit.

"Stress" can become so great that it can cause you to react in ways that you really do not desire or have little control over.

Let's look at the example in Romans 7:14-21 to see how Paul struggled in his ***"Stress Situation"*** through the **"Warfare of his Mind"** for ***Step No. 3.***

❑ <u>EXAMPLE 1</u> – <u>PAUL'S WARFARE</u>

The Apostle Paul was forced into situation(s) that he did not want to be in and, it caused him to become an irritated and ***"frustrated"*** individual. He found himself

A GUIDELINE FOR SOLVING AND COPING WITH STRESS SITUATIONS

"GUIDELINE STEPS"

- ☐ **STEP NO. 3 - EFFECTS OF THE STRESS**
- ☐ **EXAMPLE 1 - PAUL'S WARFARE (cont'd)**

"frustrated" by what he did not want to do, and he said, it was keeping him from doing the good that the law of God commanded him to do, and he found that his spirit was overcome by the ***"Effect(s) of the "Stress"*** within him and seeing the ***"Effect(s)"*** that the ***"Stress"*** was having on him, Paul sought to ***"Eliminate and Change"*** the ***"Stress."***

When you find yourself ***"Stressed"*** by the things you do not want to do and these things are keeping you from doing the things you want to do then, the ***"Effect(s)"*** of the ***"Stress"*** is beginning to have a harmful effect on you.

After you have recognized the ***"Effect(s) the Stress is having on you"*** and you ***"Seek for Ways to Change the***

A GUIDELINE FOR SOLVING AND COPING WITH STRESS SITUATIONS

"GUIDELINE STEPS"

❑ STEP NO. 3 - EFFECTS OF THE STRESS

❑ EXAMPLE 1 - PAUL'S WARFARE (cont'd)

Stress" while searching for a **"Solution"** to change your problem, look for things you can change that will reduce or eliminate your ***"Stress"*** for instance, **"YOU"** because, the ***"Guideline"*** suggests changing **"YOURSELF"** which is what the Apostle Paul did because you may not be able to change the ***"Stress Situation(s)"*** that exists outside of yourself.

Paul said when he recognized the ***"Shortcoming(s)"*** and ***"Inability(ies)"*** within himself, and when he realized the ***"Effect(s)"*** the ***"Stress"*** was having on him he decided that the **"Solution"** to his ***"Stress Situation(s)"*** was to be ***"Transformed by the renewing of his mind[10]"*** because, he believed it would lead him to solving his ***"Stress Situation(s)."*** What Paul was speaking of here

A GUIDELINE FOR SOLVING AND COPING WITH STRESS SITUATIONS

"GUIDELINE STEPS"

- **STEP NO. 3 - <u>EFFECTS OF THE STRESS</u>**
- **<u>EXAMPLE 1</u> - <u>PAUL'S WARFARE</u> (cont'd)**

was making an "**<u>internal</u>**" change within himself, a change in his "thoughts" which would be ***"Transformed by the renewing of his mind."*** Paul knew that ***"Transforming his mind"*** to look at his situation(s) in a different frame of mind to help him react to his ***"Stress Situation(s)"*** in a more positive way would be the "**Solution**" to eliminate, change, and reduce the intensity of his ***"Stress"*** therefore, Paul decided he would have to be ***"Transformed."***

Like the Apostle Paul, when you learn to ***"Transform"*** your "thinking" by the ***"renewing of your mind,"*** you will begin to view and respond to your ***"Stress Situation(s)"*** in a more positive way. Then, when you ***"Seek for Ways to Change Your Stress Situation(s),"*** you

A GUIDELINE FOR SOLVING AND COPING WITH STRESS SITUATIONS

"GUIDELINE STEPS"

- ❑ **STEP NO. 3 - EFFECTS OF THE STRESS**
- ❑ **EXAMPLE 1 - PAUL'S WARFARE (cont'd)**

should consider changing "**YOURSELF**" because, you may not be able to change the ***"Stress Situation(s)"*** that exists outside yourself because, the ***"Stress Situation(s)"*** that exists outside of yourself is not always easily changed, nor are they easily eliminated.

Now, to substantiate Paul's decision of ***"Transforming his Mind"*** through the "theory of ***"The Transformation of the Mind"*** the ***"Guideline"*** advises you to go to ***"Step No. 4"*** and ***"Seek Ways to Change the Stress"*** because, there is a "**Solution**" to change your problem.

Let's look now at ***"Step No 4" "Seeking Ways to Change the Stress"*** using two different examples, one dealing with a **"Positive"** form of **"Thinking"** and, the other dealing with a **"Negative"** form of **"Thinking."**

A GUIDELINE FOR SOLVING AND COPING WITH STRESS SITUATIONS

"GUIDELINE STEPS"

- **STEP NO. 4 – <u>SEEKING WAYS TO CHANGE THE STRESS THROUGH TRANSFORMATION OF THE MIND</u>**

- **<u>EXAMPLE 1</u> – <u>PAUL'S TEST AND TRIALS</u> – <u>THROUGH POSITIVE THINKING</u>**

Through all of the Apostle Paul his tests and trials, he tells us that he has learned that ***"In whatsoever state he found himself in to be therewith content.***[11]" You may ask, "How did the Apostle Paul accomplish this contentment?

He did it through the ***"Transformation of the Mind.***[12]***"*** Paul decided to think more **"Positively"** and, not **"Negatively"** about his ***"Stress Situation(s)"*** and, he was ***"Transformed"*** in his mind from a **"Negative"** form of **"Thinking"** to a **"Positive"** form of

A GUIDELINE FOR SOLVING AND COPING WITH STRESS SITUATIONS

"GUIDELINE STEPS"

❑ STEP NO. 4 – <u>SEEKING WAYS TO CHANGE THE STRESS THROUGH TRANSFORMATION OF THE MIND</u>

"Thinking" about his ***"Stress Situation(s)"*** and, Paul's mind was ***"Transformed"*** about how he would react to his ***"Stress Situation(s)."***

❑ <u>EXAMPLE 2</u> - DAVID'S RIVALRIES THROUGH NEGATIVE THINKING (cont'd)

When we consider one of David's Rivalries before he became King, David proved the ***"Transformation of the Mind"*** to be an effective method in his test and trials.

During the time of David's exile from his countrymen before he became King, David fled from the face of King Saul who was trying to take his life, and he decided to take refuge among King Achish, who was one of the Israelites enemies. Now, when the servants

A GUIDELINE FOR SOLVING AND COPING WITH STRESS SITUATIONS

"GUIDELINE STEPS"

❑ **STEP NO. 4 - SEEKING WAYS TO CHANGE THE STRESS - THROUGH THE TRANSFORMATION OF THE MIND**

❑ **EXAMPLE 2 - DAVID'S RIVALRIES THROUGH NEGATIVE THINKING (cont'd)**

of King Achish informed the King that David was that person that the children of Israel had praised in song as the one who had slain his 10,000 in comparison to Saul's 1,000 and this declaration made David begin to feel that he was in danger.

So, looking at the dilemma that David felt he was now faced with, he began to view his situation with **"Negative" "Thoughts"** of fear, and David's **"Thoughts"** caused him to react to his situation in a very peculiar and irrational way. David **"Thought"** that, because of the tidings of the King's servants he was

A GUIDELINE FOR SOLVING AND COPING WITH STRESS SITUATIONS

"GUIDELINE STEPS"

- ❑ **STEP NO. 4 - <u>SEEKING WAYS TO CHANGE THE STRESS - THROUGH THE TRANSFORMATION OF THE MIND</u>**

- ❑ **<u>EXAMPLE 2</u> - DAVID'S RIVALRIES THROUGH NEGATIVE THINKING (cont'd)**

now in danger, and in order to save himself from possible death at the hand of King Achish he would have to react like a "mad man" so, David began acting insane. David did not think in this manner when he first came into the presence of King Achish but, the tidings of the King's servants changed the **"Thoughts"** of David's mind, and the **"Stress (fear)"** that he felt within himself caused him to respond to his situation in a **"Negative"** way.

Although David's thinking about his situation caused a **"Negative"** reaction within him, and it ***"Transformed"***

A GUIDELINE FOR SOLVING AND COPING WITH STRESS SITUATIONS

"GUIDELINE STEPS"

- ❑ **STEP NO. 4 - SEEKING WAYS TO CHANGE THE STRESS - THROUGH THE TRANSFORMATION OF THE MIND**

- ❑ **EXAMPLE 2 - DAVID'S RIVALRIES THROUGH NEGATIVE THINKING (cont'd)**

his thinking from a **"Positive"** frame of mind to a **"Negative"** frame of mind, nevertheless, David was still ***"Transformed"*** in his **"thinking."** Though David's thoughts changed from a **"Positive"** to a **"Negative"** form of thinking about his ***"Stress Situation(s),"*** he did what he **"Thought"** would eliminate the danger, and he was still able to free himself from his ***"Stress Situation."***

In these examples of the Apostle Paul and David, the shepherd boy, both of these individuals experienced a

A GUIDELINE FOR SOLVING AND COPING WITH STRESS SITUATIONS

"GUIDELINE STEPS"

❑ **STEP NO. 4 - <u>SEEKING WAYS TO CHANGE THE STRESS - THROUGH THE TRANSFORMATION OF THE MIND</u> (cont'd)**

"Transformation of the Mind" to help them deal with their ***"Stress Situation(s)."***

When you seek for a **"Solution"** to change the ***"Stress Situation(s)"*** that exist ***"<u>internally</u>"*** or ***"<u>externally</u>"*** to yourself, you should consider the theory of ***"The Transformation of the Mind."*** This theory could be the **"Solution"** you need to change your ***"Stress Situation(s)"*** and, help bring about a change in **"YOU"** so you can view, react and respond to your ***"Stress Situation(s)"*** in a better way.

So, after you have found a **"Solution"** to change your ***"Stress Situation(s),"*** the ***"Guideline"*** advises one to

A GUIDELINE FOR SOLVING AND COPING WITH STRESS SITUATIONS

"GUIDELINE STEPS"

❑ STEP NO. 5 - <u>PRACTICE THE CHANGE THROUGH THE THEORY OF THE INCLINATION OF THE MIND</u>

follow the advice in ***"Step No. 5" "Practice the Change"*** so things can get better.

To **"Practice a Change"** in you, you must **"Put the Change"** into practice" and be willing to perform it and let nothing stop you from **"Practicing the Change"** because, in your **'Change'** you become a new **"YOU"** in mind and thought.

As you **"Put the Change"** into practice, you learn through the Word of God "what must be," "what should be," and "what has to be done" to create a new you as you learn how to cope with your ***"Stress Situation(s)."*** Then, as you learn how to apply the ***"Guideline's"*** instructions to the Word of God to help

A GUIDELINE FOR SOLVING AND COPING WITH STRESS SITUATIONS

"GUIDELINE STEPS"

❑ STEP NO. 5 - PRACTICE THE CHANGE THROUGH THE THEORY OF THE INCLINATION OF THE MIND (cont'd)

bring about a **'Change'** in **'YOU'** one of the things you'll learn is to ***"set your affection on things above and not on things on the earth.***[13]"

Now one of the definitions given for the word ***'affection'*** is the ***"Inclination of the Mind.***[14]***"*** The ***"Inclination of the Mind"*** is simply the ***"deviation of your mind"*** from whatever you are dwelling or focusing on. It is also a **"particular disposition"**[15] (***temperament, nature, character, constitution or, makeup***)" of your **"Mind or Character.*"***

For instance, when you ***"deviate or incline your mind"*** from your ***"Stress Situation(s)"*** by placing your **"Mind"** and your **"affection"** on more positive things then, the

A GUIDELINE FOR SOLVING AND COPING WITH STRESS SITUATIONS

"GUIDELINE STEPS"

❑ STEP NO. 5 - PRACTICE THE CHANGE THROUGH THE THEORY OF THE INCLINATION OF THE MIND

problem of your ***"Stress Situation(s)"*** may no longer seem a problem because, by ***"deviating or inclining your mind"*** from the ***"Stress Situation(s)"*** and placing your **"Mind" and "affection"** on other things hopefully, this will change the **"Disposition of your Mind"** from a **"Negative"** frame of mind to a **"Positive"** frame of mind, and hopefully you won't see your ***"Stress Situation(s)"*** as a problem but, you will view it as just another situation.

The ***"Inclination of the Mind"*** like the ***"Transformation of the Mind"*** is not always an easy method to practice when dealing with a ***"Stress Situation(s)"*** but, it

A GUIDELINE FOR SOLVING AND COPING WITH STRESS SITUATIONS

"GUIDELINE STEPS"

- ❑ **STEP NO. 5 - PRACTICE THE CHANGE THROUGH THE THEORY OF THE INCLINATION OF THE MIND**

certainly is a successful method of freeing the ***"Mind"*** from the burdensome weight of ***stressful*** thoughts. Let's continue examining the theory of ***"The Inclination of the Mind"*** through an example dealing with ***"Relationships"*** which at times can be ***"Stressful."***

- ❑ **EXAMPLE 1 – RELATIONSHIPS**

Using the theory of ***"The Inclination of the Mind"*** let's say you have a male friend named Harry and Harry has suddenly become attracted to another female named Sheliya. Now, you have been noticing that Harry is always preoccupied with the presence of Sheliya and, you have suddenly become ***"Stressed"*** with Harry's preoccupation.

A GUIDELINE FOR SOLVING AND COPING WITH STRESS SITUATIONS

"GUIDELINE STEPS"

❑ STEP NO. 5 - PRACTICE THE CHANGE THROUGH THE THEORY OF THE INCLINATION OF THE MIND

❑ EXAMPLE 1 – RELATIONSHIPS

Using the theory of ***"The Inclination of the Mind,"*** if you can ***"incline or deviate your mind"*** away from Harry or Sheliya and, set your ***"affection"*** on more important things then, Harry and Sheliya won't become a ***"Stress Situation"*** for you, and you will begin to view the situation of Harry's preoccupation through a **'Change'** in the ***"disposition of your mind"*** then, Sheliya and Harry won't matter because, you will begin to see Sheliya and Harry in a ***"Transformed"*** state of mind, and Sheliya and Harry won't be a problem. But, if you can't ***"deviate or incline your mind"*** away from Sheliya

A GUIDELINE FOR SOLVING AND COPING WITH STRESS SITUATION

"GUIDELINE STEPS"

- **STEP NO. 5 - <u>PRACTICE THE CHANGE THROUGH THE THEORY OF THE INCLINATION OF THE MIND</u>**

- **<u>EXAMPLE 1</u> - <u>RELATIONSHIPS</u>**

or Harry and set your ***"affection"*** on other things then, Sheliya and Harry will matter but, it can be done.

Let's look at another example dealing with the theory of ***"The Inclination of the Mind"*** this time we will use one of the Apostle Paul's situations that he dealt with in the book of Acts.

- **<u>EXAMPLE 2</u> – <u>PAUL'S COMMISSION – ACTS 9:1-31</u>**

In the account of the book of Acts, it informs us that, the Apostle Paul was a forceful enemy against the disciples of Christ, and he went about persecuting as many Christians as he could find.

A GUIDELINE FOR SOLVING AND COPING WITH STRESS SITUATION

"GUIDELINE STEPS"

- **STEP NO. 5 - <u>PRACTICE THE CHANGE THROUGH THE THEORY OF THE INCLINATION OF THE MIND</u>**

- **<u>EXAMPLE 2</u> – <u>PAUL'S COMMISSION – ACTS 9:1-31</u> (cont'd)**

So, because of Paul's hatred towards the Christians, he went to the High Priest to obtain letters from him to give him the authority to bind in chains anyone believing on the name of Jesus. One day while Paul was on the road to Damascus to persecute some of the disciples he was struck down with blindness. Then, Paul heard a voice speaking to him asking him "why are you persecuting me" and Paul said, "Who are You Lord?" Paul was informed that the voice he heard was that of Jesus, and Paul suddenly found himself dealing with a ***"Stress Situation."***

A GUIDELINE FOR SOLVING AND COPING WITH STRESS SITUATION

"GUIDELINE STEPS"

- ❑ **STEP NO. 5 - <u>PRACTICE THE CHANGE THROUGH THE THEORY OF THE INCLINATION OF THE MIND</u>**

- ❑ **<u>EXAMPLE 2</u> - <u>PAUL'S COMMISSION – ACTS 9:1-31</u> (cont'd)**

After Christ revealed to Paul who he was, Paul realized the reason for his sudden blindness, and he asked the Lord ***"what would he have him to do?"*** And God informed Paul what he wanted him to do and, Paul said, he "straightway" meaning 'at once' began to do what the Lord instructed him to do and, he zealously and eagerly performed the Lord's instruction. When Paul encountered a ***"Stress Situation"*** on the road to Damascus that he had not anticipated encountering, it compelled him to ***"Incline his mind"*** away from the **'Christians'** he was out to persecute, and to rethink

A GUIDELINE FOR SOLVING AND COPING WITH STRESS SITUATION

"GUIDELINE STEPS"

❑ **STEP NO. 5 - <u>PRACTICE THE CHANGE THROUGH THE THEORY OF THE INCLINATION OF THE MIND</u>**

❑ **<u>EXAMPLE 2</u> – <u>PAUL'S COMMISSION – ACTS 9:1-31</u> (cont'd)**

the things he was about to do, and to positively considered the Words and instruction of God. Through the Apostle Paul's unexpected encounter with Christ on the road to Damascus he experienced a change in himself through the ***"Transformation of the Mind"*** and, Paul was ***"Transformed"*** in his ***"Thinking"*** and, this **"Change"** compelled him to reconsider the things he was about to do, and as he considered the instruction of God, and the ***"Inclination of his Mind"*** away from the Christians it brought about a **"Change"** in him. Paul was changed through the ***"Transformation and***

A GUIDELINE FOR SOLVING AND COPING WITH STRESS SITUATION

"GUIDELINE STEPS"

- ❑ **STEP NO. 5 - <u>PRACTICE THE CHANGE THROUGH THE THEORY OF THE INCLINATION OF THE MIND</u>**

- ❑ **<u>EXAMPLE 2</u> – <u>PAUL'S COMMISSION – ACTS 9:1-31</u> (cont'd)**

Inclination of his Mind" and this change in Paul's **"mind"** was the **"Solution"** Paul needed to ***"Transform"*** himself from a **"Negative"** to a **"Positive"** mindset he had towards the Christians, and Paul put the **"Solution"** of this change into **"Practice,"** and he experienced a **"Change"** in his ***"Thinking."*** Then, Paul consecrated, dedicated, and devoted himself wholly to making this new **"Change"** in himself and, instead of continuing his pursuit of the Christians as an adversary against them, Paul continued his pursuit of the Christians as a fellow-yoke servant with them.

A GUIDELINE FOR SOLVING AND COPING WITH STRESS SITUATIONS

"GUIDELINE STEPS"

- **STEP NO. 5 - PRACTICE THE CHANGE THROUGH THE THEORY OF THE INCLINATION OF THE MIND**

- **EXAMPLE 2 – PAUL'S COMMISSION – ACTS 9:1-31 (cont'd)**

In many of the Apostle Paul's Christian journeys in life, Paul discovered a **"Solution"** to help him change his many ***"Stress Situation(s)."*** He realized that the answer to his ***"Stress Situation(s)"*** was the ***"Transformation and the Inclination of his mind"*** away from his ***"Stress Situation(s)"*** and Paul decided that he would consecrate, dedicate, and devote himself wholly to making this "**Change** in himself."

Though the Apostle Paul found himself in the midst of many ***"Stress Situations,"*** Paul accepted the ***"Stress Situation(s)"*** that he had to deal with through the

A GUIDELINE FOR SOLVING AND COPING WITH STRESS SITUATIONS

"GUIDELINE STEPS"

- **STEP NO. 5 - PRACTICE THE CHANGE THROUGH THE THEORY OF THE INCLINATION OF THE MIND**

- **EXAMPLE 2 – PAUL'S COMMISSION – ACTS 9:1-31 (cont'd)**

"Transformation and Inclination of his Mind," and he ***"Put the Change"*** **"into Practice"** and he ***"Transformed"*** his mind from the way he thought about his ***"Stress Situation(s)."***

Paul could not change the ***"Stress Situation(s)"*** he had to deal with in his life, so, instead of "mentally and emotionally" continuing stressfully against the ***"Stress Situation(s)"*** Paul continued gladly with the ***"Stress Situation(s)"*** through a **"Change"** in his mind. Then, Paul's weakness to deal with his ***"Stress Situation(s)"*** became strength through God by way of the **"Change"**

A GUIDELINE FOR SOLVING AND COPING WITH STRESS SITUATIONS

"GUIDELINE STEPS"

- **STEP NO. 5 - PRACTICE THE CHANGE THROUGH THE THEORY OF THE INCLINATION OF THE MIND**

- **EXAMPLE 2 – PAUL'S COMMISSION - ACTS 9:1-31 (cont'd)**

in his mind. The Apostle Paul realized that he could not always change or eliminate the ***"Stress Situation(s)"*** he encountered in his life and, God did not always allow his ***"Stress Situation(s)"*** to be removed.

So, like the Apostle Paul you may find that you may not be able to always change the ***"Stress Situation(s)*** that exists in your life but, like Paul, you can seek God's help to change your reaction and response to the ***"Stress Situation(s)"*** you encounter in your life so that, through the ***"Transformation and Inclination of the Mind"*** you can learn how to cope with your ***"Stress Situation(s)"*** as well.

A GUIDELINE FOR SOLVING AND COPING WITH STRESS SITUATIONS

"GUIDELINE STEPS"

- **STEP NO. 5 - PRACTICE THE CHANGE THROUGH THE THEORY OF THE INCLINATION OF THE MIND**

- **EXAMPLE 2 – PAUL'S COMMISSION – ACTS 9:1-31 (cont'd)**

In dealing with his ***"Stress Situation(s),"*** the Apostle Paul ***"Recognized the Problem,*** he ***Acknowledge the Existence of the Stress Situation(s)"*** in his life as well as, the ***"Shortcomings*** and ***"Inability(ies)"*** within himself, and he sought for the ***"Whereabouts of his Problem"*** because of the ***"Effect(s)*** the Stress was having on him."

Then Paul Sought for a **"Solution"** to change his problem(s) and with diligence, eagerness, and gladness Paul consecrated, dedicated and, devoted himself wholly to putting that **"Solution"** into **"Practice."**

A GUIDELINE FOR SOLVING AND COPING WITH STRESS SITUATIONS

"GUIDELINE STEPS"

❑ <u>EXAMPLE 2</u> – <u>PAUL'S COMMISSION – ACTS 9:1-31</u> (cont'd)

CONCLUSION

Like the Apostle Paul as you seek to deal with your life's ***"Stress Situation(s)"*** that you may encounter in your life and, as you seek to free yourself from your ***"Stress Situation(s)"*** and eliminate the ***"frustration"*** that you have to suffer and cope with, just as the Apostle Paul had to ***"Recognize the Problem and Acknowledge the Existence of a Stress Situation existing in his life,"*** the ***'<u>first</u>'*** thing you will have to do is to ***"Recognize the Problem and Acknowledge the Existence of a Stress Situation(s) existing in your life,"*** and ***"Seek the Whereabouts of the Problem"*** to determine where your ***"Stress"*** is coming from, and look at the ***"<u>Effect(s)</u> the Stress is having on you,"*** and how it may be affecting

A GUIDELINE FOR SOLVING AND COPING WITH STRESS SITUATIONS

"GUIDELINE STEPS"

CONCLUSION (cont'd)

❑ **EXAMPLE 2** – **PAUL'S COMMISSION – ACTS 9:1-31 (cont'd)**

your attitude and the way you view things in your life, and just like the Apostle Paul, you should go on to ***"Seek Ways to Change the Stress"*** and consider the possibility of ***"Changing Yourself."***

So, as you search to find a way to change, eliminate, or reduce the ***"Stress"*** in your life, you should learn how to apply the ***"Guideline's"*** instructions to the Word of God to find the **"Solution"** you need to **"Change"** your ***"Stress Situation(s)."*** Then, ***"Practice the Change"*** by putting the **"Solution"** of the **"Change"** into action, and as you seek to deal with the ***"Stress Situation(s)"*** that exist in your life, it is my prayer that God will help you to better understand ***"How to Cope with your Stress Situation(s)"*** instead of ignoring it so you can learn

A GUIDELINE FOR SOLVING AND COPING WITH STRESS SITUATIONS

"GUIDELINE STEPS"

CONCLUSION (cont'd)

how to dedicate and devote yourself wholly to ***"Practicing the Change"*** in order to free yourself from your ***"Stress Situation(s)."***

"Then they cry unto the LORD in their trouble, and he saveth them out of their distresses…."
(Psalm 107:19-20)

"And this is the confidence that we have in him, that, if we ask anything according to his will, he heareth us: And if we know that he hears us, whatsoever we ask, we know that we have the petitions that we desired of him."
(1 John 5:14-15)

GUIDELINE QUESTIONS

1. **RECOGNIZE YOUR STRESS PROBLEM AND ACKNOWLEDGE ITS EXISTENCE.**

Q. Are there any "Stress" problems going on in your life? Take a moment and write down the "Stress" problems you are dealing with.

____

____

____

____

____

____

____

____

____

____

GUIDELINE QUESTIONS

2. **SEEK THE WHEREABOUTS OF YOUR STRESS PROBLEM.**

   Q. Ask yourself the question, "Where is my Stress coming from?"

GUIDELINE QUESTIONS

3. LOOK AT THE EFFECTS OF YOUR STRESS.

Q. What are the Effects that the Stress is having on You? List those "Effects"

____

____

____

____

____

____

____

____

____

____

____

GUIDELINE QUESTIONS

4. **SEEK WAYS TO CHANGE YOUR STRESS.**

   Q. What can you do to change your "Stress" Problem(s)? Take the time to ask God what you can do to change your "Stress.

GUIDELINE QUESTIONS

5. PRACTICE THE CHANGE.

Q. Once you have determined what you can do to change your "Stress," make a list of what you should do to "Practice That Change."

REFERENCES

Quote By: Will Smith, American Actor. Retrieved from:
https://www.azquotes.com/quote/276573?ref=heart

Preface: Hembree, Ron, 1978, Fruit of the Spirit, pp. 55 and 57

*Medical News Today; (**Stress:** Why does it happen and how to manage it 11/28/17. By: Adam Felman).

*(How Stress happens and how to manage it; Medical News Today article).

**<u>How-Do-Your-Values-Impact-You-At-Work-Or-In-Your-Business.</u>

**(How today's businesses Are helping employees cope with Stress).

***Christians and Stress -
Pros + Cons of Stress for a Christian - Pursue God
https://www.youtube.com/watch?v=2Opg02WAbpU; https://youtu.be/oz0hsbLBReE

****Lack of Fulfillment, APA Coping with Stress at Work.

REFERENCES

How do your values impact you at work. Retrieved from: http://makinithappen.co.uk/Articles/How-Do-Your-Values-Impact-You-At-Work-Or-In-Your-Business.html

Managing Stress and Overcoming Anxiety; Video with Dr. David and Linda Hager.

Video, "Silent Frustration." By: Bishop T. D. Jakes (n.d.).

FOOTNOTES

1/A 'stimulus' is an agent or factor that provokes interest, enthusiasm, or excitement; and it is something that encourages an activity or a process to begin, increase, or develop.

2/Poverty in this sense refers to the absence of material and physical necessities for comfort.

3/A 'stimulus' is an agent or factor that provokes interest, enthusiasm, or excitement; and it is something that encourages an activity or a process to begin, increase, or develop.

4/1 Corinthian 12:7

5/2 Peter 1:2-3

6/Romans 7:24 (Read the Book of Acts for a Compilation of Paul's life).

7/2 Corinthian 4:8-9

8/Romans 7:15-21

9/Romans 7:19-23

10/Romans 12:2

11/Philippians 4:11

FOOTNOTES (cont'd)

12/Romans 12:2

13/Colossians 3:2

14/A bending of the mind (Merriam-Webster Dictionary)

15/A disposition or state of mind or body (Dictionary.com); https://en.wikipedia.org/wiki/Affection

16/James 1:3-4 (GNT-Good News Translation)

All scriptures are taken from the King James Version except where noted.

AUTOBIOGRAPHY

I was born and raised in the Washington, DC area and, educated in the District of Columbia public school system. As the youngest of six children, I grew up in a family of four sisters and one brother.

In my early childhood years starting around age four or five, many of my joyful childhood days were during the times when my father would gather all the family together after family dinner, and he would entertain us by playing various musical sounds on his harmonica, as well as, entertain us with his little Wooden-Stringed toy he made and called Black-Sambo, and he would create various little musical performances to entertain us.

These times with my father and family were some of the most wonderful times and memories of my life, and my family was filled with a lot of joy and happy days that I cherished as a child but, a few years later after the death of my father those fun-filled days began to cease. Many changes took place in my childhood and sadness, depression, heartache, and pain began to be my constant companions.

In my growing up years as a youth and teen I was very quiet and somewhat shy. I had very few friends and often found myself alone. As the youngest in the family, I began experiencing days of sibling bossiness, and I became the object of some of my sibling's negative remarks and criticism. These were the times that sadden me the most and I began to feel rejected, alone, and acquainted with much heartache and sadness in my life, and I found that dealing with people became very stressful and frustrating for me.

There were times in my life when I just wanted to get away from people and my family to stop the heartache I felt because of the criticism and negative attitudes expressed towards me. I even thought about moving away or joining a convent just to get away from people, and life's ills, and the heartache and sadness I constantly felt.

In my adult years, I was employed with the Federal Government, in Washington, DC and I worked in various Secretarial, Administrative and Staff Assistant positions. During my employment with the Federal Government, I dealt with continual displacement from one position to the next, and working for excessive micro-management mangers, I experienced so much Stress for so many years dealing with these domineering and overbearing managers.

During my adult years, as I constantly interacted more and more with people, observing them and their individual personalities, and dealing with the expression of their opinions, their concepts, and views, this caused me to become very observant of people and their behavior, personality, and character and I found that life can bring all kinds of frustration and Stress that made life with some people very difficult for me, and after dealing with so much Stress in my employment life, I decided after 47 years of government service, I had enough and in 2014, I decided to retire.

After retirement, I decided to continue with my long-time goal of obtaining my Bachelor's Degree, and in August of 2019 I was able to obtain my Bachelor of Science Degree in 'Christian Counseling and Psychology' from Crown College in St. Bonifacius, Minnesota.

Through my life situations, as I began to deal more and more with people and their attitude and personality, with financial and human life situations, I began to realize how **"Stress"** can be developed in a person's life and how it can create all kinds of emotions and life problems, and during these times, I learned through many of my life experiences that, life can hold an abundance of unexpected life situations that one may not be able to avoid, and I realized that, no matter where I go, or what I do in life, no matter who I interact with, there can always be the possibility that **"Stress"** will be created in my life but, learning how to deal with that **"Stress"** was the key to a more Stress free life.

A Quote By:

Actor 'Will Smith'

"Throughout life people will make you mad, disrespect You and treat you bad.
Let God deal with the things they do, cause hate in your heart will consume you too."

To God Be The Glory!